PoOP CoLLeCTORS, ARMPIT SNIFFeRS, AND MORE:

THE YUCKY JOBS BOOK

and Virginia Silverstein
Laura Silverstein Nunn

Illustrated
by Gerald Kelley

Library of Congress Cataloging-in-Publication Data

Silverstein, Alvin.
    Poop collectors, armpit sniffers, and more : the yucky jobs book / by Alvin Silverstein, Virginia Silverstein, and Laura Silverstein Nunn.
        p. cm. — (Yucky science)
    Summary: "Explores various 'yucky' jobs, including crime-scene cleaning, pig farming, snake milking, and more"—Provided by publisher.
    Includes bibliographical references and index.
    ISBN 978-0-7660-3316-0
    1. Hazardous occupations—Juvenile literature. 2. Sanitation—Juvenile literature. 3. Body fluids—Juvenile literature. 4. Odors—Juvenile literature. I. Silverstein, Virginia B. II. Nunn, Laura Silverstein. III. Title.
    HD7262.S54 2011
    331.702—dc22
                    2009021273

Printed in the United States of America

062010 Lake Book Manufacturing Inc., Melrose Park, IL

10 9 8 7 6 5 4 3 2 1

Illustration Credits: © 2009 Gerald Kelley, www.geraldkelley.com
Cover Illustration: © 2009 Gerald Kelley, www.geraldkelley.com
Photo Credits: ANT Photo Library/Photo Researchers, Inc., p. 41; Associated Press, pp. 15, 19, 30, 40; © Britta Kasholm-Tengve/iStockphoto.com, p. 21 (top); Dennis Kunkel Microscopy, Inc./Visuals Unlimited, Inc., p. 8; Hulton Archive/Getty Images, p. 21 (bottom); Shutterstock, pp. 12, 25, 35; © Valeriy Kirsanov/iStockphoto.com, p. 43.

Enslow Publishers, Inc.
40 Industrial Road
Box 398
Berkeley Heights, NJ 07922
USA
    http://www.enslow.com

CONTENTS

What's Yucky?

Vomit . . . slime . . . blood and guts . . . rotting garbage . . . a squishy pile of dog poop . . . Just thinking of things like these can make you exclaim, "Eew, gross!" Actually seeing, smelling, or touching yucky things can make you feel like throwing up.

Most people try to avoid yucky things. You probably do, too. But many people work every day with things you might think are yucky.

Would you take a job where you had to handle garbage or wade through rivers of poop? Would you work in a place so stinky that people hold their noses as they drive by? What about a job where you were often bitten or stung or at risk of catching a deadly disease?

Lots of people do take jobs like these. Maybe they just don't mind things that seem yucky to you. Or they might be bothered by them at first, but then get used to them. It's lucky for the rest of us that there are people who can handle all sorts of jobs.

Think about what the world would be like if garbage just piled up with nobody to haul it away! Many dirty, stinky, or dangerous jobs are absolutely necessary to keep us healthy and safe.

In this book you'll read about some of the yucky (but important) jobs people do.

CHAPTER ONE

Stinky Jobs

STINKY PITS

How good is your sniffer? Every day, you are bombarded with smells. Most of the time you don't even notice them—unless the smells are really good, like chocolate chip cookies baking in the oven. Or you might notice really yucky smells, such as rotting garbage in a Dumpster.

Would you believe that some people have jobs that depend on their keen sense of smell?

Why Do Armpits Stink?

One word: bacteria. Bacteria are microscopic organisms. They live on your body all the time. Most don't bother you at all. Some of them make you sick. Others just make you *stink*. That's what happens when armpits get smelly. When people exercise, for example, their armpits may get sweaty. Bacteria eat sweat chemicals. Then they grow, multiply, and give off a really stinky smell.

These bacteria, here magnified over 10,000 times by a microscope, can cause body odors. (This photo has been artificially colored.)

They are odor testers. But these people don't spend all day smelling things like roses or chocolate candy. Part of their job is to smell people's armpits!

Odor testers work for companies that make deodorants, mouthwash, and other products used to help cover up or remove yucky smells. So how can these companies tell if a deodorant works? That's the tricky part. An odor tester has to sniff the armpits of sweaty strangers! It's not too bad if the deodorant does a good job covering up the stink—and leaves a nice perfumy smell. But if all the tester smells is stinky sweat—yuck! That's a clear sign that the product is not ready to be sold in stores.

P.U.! STINKY FEET!

Do you have stinky feet? Many people do. So can you imagine what it must be like to be a foot doctor? A foot doctor, known as a podiatrist, handles people's bare feet all day long! Feet can get really sweaty trapped inside shoes for so many hours at a time. Bacteria grow and multiply very quickly in dark, moist places, like sweaty shoes. So by the end of the day, P.U.! Stinky feet!

What could be worse than smelly feet if you're a podiatrist? How about foot sores? People visit the podiatrist for all sorts of foot problems. Their feet may be covered with strange-looking lumps and bumps, such as warts, corns, and bunions. Or they may have a nasty rash caused by a fungus. Feet may bleed while the doctor is working on them, or sores may ooze yucky stuff. Of course, a podiatrist wears a protective mask and gloves. These don't help much with the smell, but they do keep germs from spreading when the doctor handles a patient's feet.

Some people think that feet are just plain yucky. If you're one of them, you probably don't want to be a podiatrist. To be a foot doctor, you really have to love feet—warts and all!

PIGGING OUT

What's it like to be a pig farmer? You probably imagine it as really messy and stinky. Are pigs really as dirty as people think they are? That depends. They do like to roll around in mud, but that's mainly to keep cool. (A coating of mud protects their skin from sunburn, too.) Pigs will also cool off in a pool of water if one is available.

It's hard for pigs to stay clean, though, if they are kept in crowded pigpens. And on many big pig farms, the animals are kept in small cages. Their poop falls through the wire mesh floor of the cage and is flushed out into big pits. There's a lot of it! A farm with 3,000 pigs puts out as much poop as a town of 10,000 people!

With all that poop, the barns where the pigs live really stink. In fact, pig farms smell so bad that people in passing cars sometimes hold their noses as they go by.

Pigs can be very dirty because they like to roll in mud to keep cool.

What a Stink!

Pig poop smells much worse than poop from horses or cattle. That's because the food pigs eat has more protein than horse or cattle feed. When pigs digest this food, they make a lot of smelly chemicals. The bacteria living in the pigs' intestines grow and multiply, adding to the poop. By the time it plops out of the pig, it *really* stinks!

The stinky smell is often unbearable for families who live nearby. That's why towns near pig farms have passed laws to control pig raising and poop storage.

Pig poop not only smells bad, it is actually dangerous. Many pig farmers develop breathing problems. They may even develop serious lung diseases, such as pneumonia and asthma. That's because the air in buildings with indoor pens is filled with dust. This is not like the dust in your home. Pig farm dust contains tiny bits of germ-filled poop. Poisonous gases also build up and make farm workers sick—some have even died.

CHAPTER TWO

Poop Patrol

A RIVER OF POOP

Have you ever wondered what's under those manhole covers scattered along streets in your neighborhood? If you had a chance to peer down one, you might notice water flowing along like a river. But this is no ordinary river. It's the sewer system.

The sewer contains all sorts of yucky stuff. Every time someone in the neighborhood flushes a toilet, the poop and pee get flushed through a system of pipes that ends up in the sewer. All that yucky stuff—the waste matter that drains into the sewer system—is called sewage.

Would you walk through a stink-filled sewer, knee-deep in sewage? If you are a sewer worker, that's exactly what you do. A sewer

Rob Smith clears away gunk in the London sewer system to keep it running smoothly.

Yikes! Sewer workers don't like to talk much while working in the sewer. If they are not wearing masks, raw sewage could splash into their mouths!

worker's job is to clear away any objects that clog up a sewer system. Often, the workers have to remove sticks and rocks that are blocking a sewer pipe. But sometimes they find some interesting things down there, such as jewelry, screwdrivers, marbles, toy cars, plastic dinosaurs, and even bicycle tires.

As if the smell and waste aren't gross enough, sewer workers need to do their job while cockroaches and rats scurry along the sewer walls—and sometimes along their clothes!

Being a sewer worker can also be dangerous. Sewage contains germs that may spread diseases. Workers may also breathe in harmful gases. They may even drown in the poop-filled waters!

YOU CLEAN WHAT?

Who wouldn't want to work at a zoo? You get to see the elephants, tigers, and monkeys

Yikes! At the Miami Metrozoo in Florida, one of the male elephants, Dahlip, produced 540 pounds (245 kilograms) of poop in a twenty-four-hour period!

whenever you want. But what if the job involved cleaning the poop out of the animals' cages or pens? This kind of job can get really stinky and pretty messy. Animal cage cleaners have to scoop up mounds of poop every day!

Scooping up poop isn't like shoveling snow. You can scoop up a mound of snow and throw it over your shoulder. You don't want to do that with poop or you will surely get splattered! After cage cleaners scoop the poop, they carefully carry it away.

Cleaning cages is a messy, smelly job. It can be hard and sometimes dangerous work. Cage cleaners do a lot of kneeling, bending, and crawling around. They may be bitten or scratched, catch diseases, or develop allergies from breathing in poop dust.

Zoos are not the only places where cage cleaners can find work. People who love animals and don't mind a dirty job can volunteer at an animal shelter. When they're not cleaning cages, they get to pet the animals. Boarding kennels, stables, and veterinary hospitals also use cage cleaners. There are plenty of jobs like this—wherever there are animals, you'll find poop!

Zoo Poop For Sale

Many zoos actually sell "zoo poo" as fertilizer. Elephants, rhinos, and other large zoo animals are fed a rich diet of plants, vegetables, and fruit. Their poop makes great plant food for vegetable, fruit, and herb gardens, as well as trees, flowers, and grass. Zoo poop has also been recycled into paper products including books, paper flowers, and Christmas ornaments. Zoos in China and Thailand sell sports statues, picture frames, fans, greeting cards, and bookmarks made from panda poop. Pandas eat bamboo, so their poop contains a lot of pulp—perfect for making paper products.

This panda-shaped souvenir sold in China is made of panda poop!

CHAPTER THREE

Dirty Jobs

CHIM-CHIMINEE

Imagine a fire crackling in a fireplace. You can see flames shooting upward and smoke rising up into the chimney. This used to be the main way to heat peoples' homes. To keep the fireplace working right, the chimneys had to be cleaned regularly. It was a really dirty job.

In the seventeenth, eighteenth, and nineteenth centuries, chimney sweeps—people who cleaned chimneys for a living—got covered head-to-toe with soot. Many people didn't wash very often in those days. Sweeps just brushed off the soot when they got home. There was so much soot that they stuffed bags with it and used them for pillows. They breathed in soot on the job and also at home, even when they slept! Those who weren't

Sweeping chimneys was historically a dirty and dangerous job. Compare the chimney sweep on the right (from the 1950's) to the modern chimney cleaner above!

Yikes! Before the twentieth century, many chimney sweeps were children as young as seven years old. The children, known as "Climbing Boys," could climb into the narrow chimneys more easily than full-grown adults.

killed on the job by falls or by getting stuck up in the chimney usually died young of lung disease. The chemicals in chimney soot can also cause cancer.

Chimney cleaning is still an important job today. When fuels—such as wood, coal, or oil—burn in a fireplace or furnace, they produce powdery black soot and sticky black gunk. The heat of the fire carries these products up the chimney. Some go out into the air. (That's why smoke from a chimney looks dark.) But bits of black stuff also stick to the inside of the chimney. Over time, they can build up and block the opening. Birds' nests and fallen bricks can also block chimneys. Then the smoke from the fire blows back into the house, which can be dangerous. The soot

inside the chimney could also catch fire—and burn down the whole house! So even today's chimneys need to be inspected and cleaned every year.

Working conditions are a lot better for today's chimney cleaners. They now use high-powered vacuum cleaners and other modern tools. They also wear protective clothing and breathe through respirators while they work. But it's still a dirty job!

HOT AND STICKY

What's so yucky about being a hot tar roofer? Two words: *hot tar!* Hot tar roofers spread tar underneath roof shingles to keep the roof from leaking when it rains or snows. But tar is not much fun to work with. It is some very sticky stuff! To give you an idea of what it's like, imagine stepping into a pool of honey on the floor and then walking around. Your shoes would be sticky with every step. Yuck! But unlike honey, tar is very dark. So not only is it sticky, it can get dark stains on your shoes and clothes.

The worst part of being a hot tar roofer, though, is that the tar is extremely hot. It may

Hot tar is mopped onto a roof. The worker needs to be very careful, or he could get burned.

be hundreds of degrees! That means it can be pretty dangerous stuff. Roofers have to carry pails of hot tar up stepladders and walk carefully across roofs. Tar may splash out of the pails. If the roofers trip or fall, they could get seriously burned. Even though the roofers wear gloves and other protective clothing, hot tar can burn right through, melting their clothes onto their skin.

Treating hot tar burns is very difficult. The sticky tar clamps onto the body. You can't remove it without removing the skin itself!

CHAPTER FOUR

Bloody Jobs

IT'S AN EMERGENCY!

Have you ever watched a TV show about doctors in the emergency room (ER)? The ambulance comes screeching to a stop in front of the emergency room doors. The patient is wheeled into the hospital. Maybe he is the victim of a car accident. The ER doctor rushes over to the patient. Blood is gushing from deep cuts in the patient's head and dripping down his face. Blood is soaking his arms and legs, as well. There's no time to waste! The ER doctor has to make smart, split-second decisions to save this person's life. It's all in a day's work.

In real life, the emergency room isn't always buzzing with nonstop action, with blood and guts everywhere. Sometimes it's quiet.

Patients may trickle in. Some may have minor problems, such as sprained ankles or small cuts that need a few stitches. But there are times when the ER can get pretty bloody and gross, especially when it involves accident victims.

Accidents can happen anywhere—whether it's a bad car crash, an accident at home while using tools, or an accident at work with a heavy machine. Sometimes people can get seriously injured. With deep wounds, a person

Yikes! If someone loses a finger in an accident, doctors may be able to reattach it. But they have to do it within twelve hours if it is kept at room temperature. A cut-off finger can last for a couple of days in a refrigerator. Either way, it should be wrapped in a damp cloth or paper towel and sealed up in a plastic bag. Placing the bag in a bag or a jar with ice can help keep the finger from going bad. The finger shouldn't actually touch the ice, though. That would damage the tissues. Soaking the finger in water is not a good idea, either. It would shrivel up.

can lose a lot of blood. They may even lose fingers, a hand, or some other body part. If you're an ER doctor, you can't get squeamish when you see blood. And you have to think fast and make good decisions—it could literally be a matter of life or death!

CALLING MR. CLEAN!

A terrible crime has been committed. On the local news, the reporter says that a man was killed in his own home. The police came and investigated the crime scene. As the family waited outside, the investigators did their jobs. They collected evidence, took samples, and looked for clues. That's routine for a murder investigation. But what happens to the house after the investigators leave? Blood may be soaked into the carpet and splattered on the walls. Who is supposed to clean up this terrible mess? It's not the job of the crime scene investigators, it's the family's!

Luckily, families can call in crime scene cleaners for help. It's true! There are companies that specialize in cleaning up crime scenes.

Crime scene cleaners wear special suits and use special equipment to make sure everything is germ-free.

By hiring crime scene cleaners, family members don't have to do the job themselves.

Cleaning up crime scenes is not an easy job. For one thing, it can get pretty gruesome. A crime scene cleaner needs a really strong stomach to handle the gore and horrible smells left by the decaying body. Another thing that makes the job difficult is that body fluids, including blood or tissue found at a crime scene, are considered dangerous because they may be infected with disease. So the cleaners must wear protective gloves, masks, and outfits. And they can't just put the stuff they remove out in the trash. Usually, they take it to be burned in a special medical waste incinerator.

Would You Believe...?
Depending on the job, crime scene cleaners may get paid up to $600 per hour!

CHAPTER FIVE

Working with the Dead

DOCTOR DETECTIVE

When a person dies, there are sometimes unanswered questions. How did the person die? Was it violent? What was the cause of death? It is the medical examiner's job to find out the answers to those questions.

A medical examiner (ME) is a medical doctor. But being an ME means you also have to do a bit of detective work. You need to look for clues and gather evidence. Are there marks on the body, such as cuts or bruises? Are there stray hairs or fibers on the body? Everything has to be recorded. The doctor must then collect hair samples, fingernails, fibers (from clothing, carpets, or other things), and anything else found on the body.

A major part of the medical examiner's job is doing autopsies. An autopsy involves cutting a body open to examine the insides. The organs may even need to be taken out. Blood and tissue samples also have to be tested. The autopsy will scientifically determine the cause of death.

Practice Makes Perfect

Young surgeons cannot practice their surgery techniques on live people. So they learn by operating on dead people. If they make a mistake no one gets hurt!

REST IN PEACE

Have you ever heard that when dead people are buried, their bodies are eaten away by worms and crawling insects? That's a really gross thought! But it's true. In fact, a dead body will start to break down even *before* it's time for the burial.

The moment a person dies, the body starts to break down. Bacteria inside the intestines multiply and start eating away at other organs. As the body rots, it begins to smell. The smell attracts flies, which lay their eggs in body openings, such as the mouth, nose, and eyes. The eggs hatch into wormlike maggots, which feed on the body. The rotting body attracts more flies, as well as beetles and mites. Soon the body is crawling with creatures.

The Making of a Mummy

The ancient Egyptians invented embalming. They did it a bit differently than we do today, however. The Egyptians first removed the internal organs and kept them in jars filled with a chemical solution. The brain was chopped up into tiny pieces using a hook, and then pulled out through the nose! The body was then treated with chemicals and left to dry for about forty days. Wrapped up in linen bandages, it became . . . a mummy!

A funeral director uses a special process called embalming to keep the body from rotting before the funeral. During the process, the funeral director puts tubes into the body and drains all body liquids. Then he fills the body with a fluid containing strong chemicals that kill bacteria and keep the body from rotting. Embalming doesn't last forever. Eventually, the dead body will start to rot—but that won't happen until long after it is buried.

ON THE ROAD AGAIN

A dead deer on the side of the road is not a pretty sight. But it's even worse when you can see the guts spilling out! Sometimes dead animals are left on the ground for days or weeks. The longer they stay there, the more time their bodies have to rot. That can be a yucky, smelly mess for anybody that lives or shops nearby. It can also be dangerous because the dead animals may be full of germs. No one would want to get anywhere close to that rotting animal—unless they're a roadkill collector. It is this person's job to drive down

streets and highways looking for roadkill—animals killed on the road by cars and trucks.

All kinds of dead animals may be found on the road, including deer, raccoons, and squirrels. Sometimes the animals haven't been there long, maybe a few hours. Other times, the bodies might have been lying outside for days. By that time, the animal's body has already started to rot. It becomes soft, and the gut might be torn open. Some of its organs might be hanging out. Flies hover over the body. Maggots and other insects munch on its insides. Vultures and foxes may also have eaten parts of the body.

Now imagine the roadkill collector having to pick the animal up and lift it onto the back of a truck. Yuck! It's not easy. Sometimes, skin falls off or guts spill out of the body. Then the collector has to pick them up separately—with gloves of course! At the same time, the smell is unbearable! We're lucky that there are people willing to do this job. By removing roadkill that might spread disease or attract other animals, they help keep the streets and roads safe.

CHAPTER SIX

Dangerous Jobs

MILKING SNAKES

If you saw a snake slithering along the ground, would you run the other way? Or would you pick it up? What if it's poisonous? It's usually not a good idea to pick up snakes.

If a snake is poisonous, its bite could be harmful, even deadly. But that doesn't stop snake milkers from doing their job. These are wildlife experts who snatch poisonous snakes from their hiding places—hopefully without getting bitten. They need to have experience in identifying and handling snakes. Snake milkers bring the snakes back to a laboratory so they can "milk" venom (poison) from their fangs. Scientists use snake venom to make anti-venom, a medicine that treats snakebite victims.

This rattlesnake is being milked for its venom.

So, how do they actually "milk" snakes? The snake milker has the snake bite through a thin, rubber-like material covering a small glass container. Biting into the material forces the snake's venom sacs (on each side of the upper jaw) to squeeze out venom into the container. The venom is later freeze-dried and packaged by staff members who wear protective masks.

Yikes! **The Australian taipan is the deadliest snake in the world. Its venom is 50 times more deadly than cobra venom.**

The chance of survival for someone who has been bitten by a taipan is only three percent. And yet, scientists can turn its deadly venom into medicine that can *save* people who have been bitten by a taipan. But the treatment is no good unless the snakebite gets treated within the hour.

Breathing in dried venom can be just as dangerous as getting bitten.

Snake milkers get only a few drops of venom from each snake. Depending on the kind of snake, hundreds of milkings may be needed to make a single dose of anti-venom. They usually keep anti-venom close by—just in case they get bitten. Most snake milkers will get bitten at some point in their career.

WHAT'S THE BUZZ?

Can you imagine getting stung by lots of bees at the same time? One is bad enough, but more than that—ouch! That's the kind of danger that beekeepers face.

While many people would probably run away from bees, it is a beekeeper's job to get up close and personal with them—*real* close! Beekeepers take care of honeybees. Honeybees are very important to farmers and orchard growers. The bees fly around gathering nectar from flowers to make honey. At the same time, the bees pick up powdery pollen and carry it from flower to flower. Tiny male cells in the pollen join with female cells inside the flower to form seeds. Without the bees' help, some flowers would not be able to make seeds to start the next generation.

Beekeepers have to wear protective suits and gloves, as well as a helmet and a veil to protect the face. Staying calm and making slow, smooth movements can also help them avoid getting stung. Most beekeepers do get

Beekeepers wear protective clothing to keep themselves from being stung too often.

Yikes! Some people are allergic to bee stings. For these people, a bee sting can be deadly. The venom in the stinger causes a serious reaction, making the breathing muscles tighten. Then the victim can't breathe and needs medical attention right away!

stung—some as many as ten times a day! A sting is a lot worse for the bee, though. The bee loses its stinger and dies from the wound.

* * * *

Do you know anyone who cleans up animal poop, picks up dead animals from the roadside, or does autopsies for a living? These jobs might sound yucky to you, but fortunately there are people willing to do them. Let's be thankful to them!

WORDS TO KNOW

autopsy The examination of a dead body to determine the cause of death.

bacteria Microscopic single-celled organisms. Some cause diseases. Others are involved in decay (rotting).

incinerator A furnace, especially for burning trash.

maggot The immature form (larva) of the housefly, commonly found in rotting garbage.

sewage Waste matter that drains into a sewer system.

soot Powdery black matter (mostly carbon) that remains after burning.

venom Poison from certain animals, such as some poisonous snakes, insects, and arachnids (spiders and scorpions).

wound A break in the skin; an injury.

FURTHER READING

Allman, Toney. *The Medical Examiner.* Farmington Hills, Mich.: Lucent Books, 2006.

Harper, Charise Mericle. *Flush! The Scoop on Poop Throughout the Ages.* New York: Little, Brown, 2007.

Malam, John. *You Wouldn't Want to Be a 19th Century Coal Miner in England!: A Dangerous Job You'd Rather Not Have.* Danbury, Conn.: Franklin Watts, 2007.

Scott, Carey. *Crime Scene Detective.* New York: DK Publishing, 2007.

INTERNET ADDRESSES

Discovery Channel. "Dirty Jobs with Mike Rowe."
<http://dsc.discovery.com/fansites/dirtyjobs/
dirtyjobs.html>
*Videos, quizzes, and dirty fun, based on the popular
TV show.*

Popular Science. "The Worst Jobs in Science, 2007."
<http://www.popsci.com/scitech/article/2007-06/
worst-jobs-science-2007>
*Want a career in science? How about whale poop collector
(follow the whales with a poop-sniffing dog), garbologist
(dig into landfills and see what was dumped), or forensic
entomologist (help solve crimes by studying blowflies,
maggots, and other bugs that like dead bodies)? Read
about yucky science jobs and the people who do them.*

INDEX